Love the Struggle to Success

By

LifeGoodenergy

THE SWEETEST OF G

There is a joy that loves gives you when you're connected with someone like you and this place of peace is where you want to be forever! The comfort and support bring on more strength than you ever can imagine. And the passion is persistence beyond any measures. Greatness my Goodness!! We soared like eagles for years!! We were paired spiritually, way beyond any physical attraction could give. Our love was everlasting! We walked through storms unharmed and never feared God's decisions. We took it day by day, allowing God to make a way out of any way. We were Victorious! A journey known by few and daily lived by us. We never failed to be great. We set standards that we lived by, and our love reminded us of that importance. It was a destiny that we couldn't deny, and it led us to an unforgettable life. Now It's All Over! I have cried in sorrow, I have cried in hurt, I have cried in pain, I have cried in memory, I have cried in peace, I have cried in joy, I have cried in happiness, but I won't cry for your return. You have lived a legendary life! You have sought God's mission and your life speaks the glory. Here's the story I'm left with, "A great lady who fought a great fight," ask me, "Will I continue to fight a good fight?" And I have been fighting a good fight ever since. A real story of Greatness!

It was our usual morning texting, but this one spoke more life in my life than ever before. It said, "Good Morning Millionaire Ma'r," and my whole life changed that day. It symbolized more than I can ever explain, and the words meant everything. There is something about a person experiencing their last days and not even thinking of death but bringing and speaking more life in others. It was an amazing journey we were on, and your part of my journey I never thought would come to an end. But one thing I know for sure, if I keep fighting a good fight, we will meet again. May you continue to rest in peace. And I'll make sure your greatness lives forever! Love You Dearly, Sweet G!

REST IN PEACE SWEET G!
In Memory of Gaynelle Perrilloux Ellis

The Introduction

Life is beautiful! But this journey of success can bring a lot struggle your way. But don't panic! Enjoy the challenges of life because these are points that you become your strongest. Take notes and go through all the obstacles like they apart of your accomplishments. Feel free and less emotional from all these situations that won't last. Take pride in knowing all the lessons of life brings you better life. And enjoy being successful before you actually are successful. You are very amazing. And your greatness is about to shine through all that rain. We only have tears of joy, now. I forever encourage you to be everything you imagined to be. No matter how easy it looks, everyone feels the pressures and pain. And the only thing makes us all different is some of us chose to keep going. You can join us now, loving the struggle to success. There is so much waiting on you. People will tell you it's a lonely road. But actually, you only have to connect with people who understand your movement. The whole team believes in you! And of course you know, "I Love The Team!"

TABLE OF CONTENTS

Success Section

THE LOVE SECTION

HOLD MY HAND

Hold my hand across the land that you been waiting to reach where the fellowship is different, I do more practicing then trying to preach
Freedom couldn't be more free; free of mind, free of speech
Free will on how you feel, good sow good reap is what I teach
To be at peace where time is not a factor when we at feast
We never in a rush, enjoying the sun moving west from out the east
How unique to be yourself in a form of good health
Because good wealth comes natural to those who don't hold back themselves
And most of all, they solve before they have problems
We do relationship maintenance so they're only situations by the time we got them
Godly patterns we tend to follow because it seems the only way
I built a relationship with happiness, so he comes around like everyday
And people wonder if they would ever see it, I tell them if you're living it ain't too late
Even my bad days seem great because I know they won't last forever
It like dealing with family sometimes it takes funerals to bring us back together
But I couldn't ask for nothing better than to live before I die
Hold my Hand across the land because I won't life pass you by

ZONE OUT ON LOVE

If only for one night, I could bring to life what I have insight
A vision of you perfect where the place and time is always right
That moment when I'm not focus on my type, but the happiness we have
With that feeling of comfort, when you smirk at me, every time you pass
Less than minutes spent, but you can see it [Love] clear as glass
I would daze all day but this picture just won't last
I won't let them bury my treasure! Cause they think you only trash
Your image may come less than a second but this feeling just won't pass
Let me shower you with joy and turn that smirk into a laugh
Let me give you back that fuel you give when I'm running out of gas
Can I buy another second until I no longer have any more cash
I'm just pursuing my love and happiness investing in a dream I have
I can tell you on my knees I care and the gift is just a symbol
For the times I can't get back to you, you'll have something to remember
Let our feelings not be hindered because our time is only a fraction in this moment
So I release my heart to you to have whenever you get lonely
I have a love for zoning, but every time you come you leave
But I have imagination attached to faith so you staying is what I believe
I am zoning, I'm zone, Zoning out on Love! WHY?
I have love for zoning

SUCH A GENTLEMAN

I'm such a gentleman that it's evident that I'm hated by my fellowmen
Because ever since I been raised by one parent
I let being a man becomes transparent
And I'm not caring what the thoughts of playing it smart
When I more focus on curing hearts that been torn apart
Raising the mark and breaking charts
I'm bringing the love back like the freedom we fought
And I don't divide them and sort, I love them all equal
Never change for game; I'm still the same through all sequels
I have respect for all people so I won't bring curse to your life
I won't bring worst to the wife, so I process thoughts
Everything twice
I'm trying to do this thing right don't caution, you safe from danger
You can fall in love with a stranger that you been knowing
You haven't notice it, but you been glowing
And as we are growing, let this love flow so deep
Even when you woke, you'll think you'll sleep
I'm so unique they think I'm a freak
Because the vibe so strong it keeps you weak
Take a peek, I'm such a gentleman

BEAUTIFUL BROKEN HEART

It's so beautiful when two broken hearts have come together
When you no longer looking for the best, you just looking for something better
Cause in the past you have been stab, sliced, and torn open
And took for granted by everybody that you thought was important
Hoping while you are floating nobody else bust your bubble
That you apart of couple with a person who has a couple
And that trouble turns to double to find out you just another number
But your innocence keeps you humble as your energy begins to slumber
This rain brings on thunder but after lighting, there is a bow
With some very pretty colors red, blue, yellow, green and purple
So just know you're special when you cry and stuck in pride
You be amaze if I wasn't there the same time you was passing by
And I usually ask him why we fall victim to love prison
But you already know there is a bigger picture to his vision
I'm sorry about that beautiful
Hi my name is Broken Heart
And I hoping we can get together one day
It's just a thought

NOW OR NEVER

Isn't real love what you want?
To travel the world with a loved companion
A man who holds his own to make sure that he takes care of his family
The feeling of security and the extra when you need it
Is this really what you want cause today you're going to meet him
But maybe you're going through something and today is not the day
And yesterday wasn't better, and tomorrow not looking great To much already upon your plate, so many excuses you can say
That you really want a good man, but today is just not the day
Maybe people just don't understand, you rather struggle by yourself
Or maybe God shouldn't listen when you pray to him for help
Or He is really fine; every relationship goes through stuff
Or maybe when you said you're tired, you really didn't have enough
No matter what the situation is, sometimes you just need a change
All men make mistakes is true they are similar but not the same
You want a gain but taking losses on an investment you guess with
Well I can be living answer key with a guarantee to help with your assessment
Yes I am a good man, some say by popular demand
Even her good loving followed by the pain couldn't force me to want to change
And that's real love; the truth, honesty, and respect
So if today is the day
Then the love you willing to give you will finally receive back

FRIENDS FOREVER

There is no weather that keeps us from being the better of together
We have seen storms last long and seemed forever
But the challenge is not strong enough and we are thick as cheddar
For us to want to deprive ourselves of being birds of feathers
Our words of friendship is words of metal
We fall in the same category pots and kettles
There aren't any soft spots where water can settle
Because we settle out the differences when things are mellow
Tell goodbye to the lies and the facts get hellos
And we always can get picked up if anyone has fell low
They say, "That's what's good friends for" when the time is needed
Steadily growing off a pledge that once was seeded
And any relationship will grow once you feed it
So don't worry about the cries because water needed
Believe me, good friends are so easy to see
And soon as you realize it, it's so easy to be
So concentrate on the love that can run so easily deep
As it reminds us of the reason that you easy keep
A friendship we once thought that would never get better
But here we are now, years later, friends forever

WHAT SHE DO TO YOU?

She gives me butterflies!
A reason to rise pass stars, fly pass mars, all just because I can
The feelings that I have for her is so unthinkable
That there is nothing in this world that can stop us
We unsinkable
Just thinking of her another chill goes through my body
Isn't it beautiful to have her mind, body, and soul and not just her body
I wish this for everybody to see love similar to this
Because this that 1 out of 352 relationships that seemed to never exist
And when we kiss her lips wrap round mines in a square to the root of my tooth
Ain't nothing safe about this love, not my hardhat, Nomex or the steel toe of my boot
She a trespasser but I won't shoot as I dance to the music of her unknown flute
So cute and sexy in my mind, the thoughts are rare
Head high like a building let the sky scrape us
We so comfortable let the wind takes us
We so in love right now I think love starting to hate us
We play fuss just because I won't allow her to do more
So I'm wondering what it is like to explore her mind while loving her core
As I'm reaching for her door, my body begins to shiver
The door is open, and that's all I ever remember Damn!

IT'S REAL LOVE?

My first time in this situation, I never thought it could have happened to me
No matter how much I tried to feel different, happiness is all I could see
Feeling like I'm out of my jurisdiction because the friction between us was of one accord
And I'm used to jumping ship before getting seasick but right now, I'm happy I'm aboard
Her feelings just pour out like Kool-Aid on a summer day
And I sip on my cup hoping these feelings don't fade away
She's amazing grace and her sound is so sweet like honey
I could hear her calling me, "Poo Bear!"
As she slowly rubbing on my tummy
Energy like the bunny and for some reason, I can go on and on
I then travel the world enough looking for a house and right now, I found a home
Hours sitting on the phone because the conversation so relaxing
As she explains what I'm wondering without her even asking
Her passion was everlasting and what she cared for was unconditioned
My feelings started getting deep and my heart started making its own decisions
With no intuition, I feel like she could be the one
Because 6 months in the relationship it still feels like it just begun
Adventurous and the chances she takes shows her courage
Because she didn't mind stepping out on faith, and starting over was nothing
She a hundred, my sunshine in the month of May
Here's a future so promising because of a choice we made today

GRANDMA'S LOVE

I love you Grandma, your lessons were priceless
Your words were the wisest, and your attitude was the nicest
And I thank you for all you have done to mold her
Because she is everything you wanted her to be like you showed her
To have days that couldn't get no colder, her life stays bright
And even at the weakest of moments, she stills had fight
And no matter what was wrong everything seems right
All she did was focus on that morning joy to make it through the night
She is what I call every man type but some of them will never get the picture
So they focus on themselves while they abuse her without even hitting her
Most women would have quickly quit, but her shell is so thicker
Always finding a sweeter taste out the sourness of a pickle
And you would think it was to be richer, but it wasn't cash that made her different
She was taught family first and her team was her vision
So she would die to see her family stay together for better
It like opening a tombstone the day that I met her
And it wasn't so much of pleasure because I wasn't sure she could revive
But no matter how the outside may have looked you couldn't change her insides
What a moment to shed tears, Thanks Grandma, for teaching my lady how to live
No matter what, Darling, always be a wife to your husband and mother to your kids

WHAT'S A QUEEN?

I smile cause I finally know what it means to have the reality aspect instead of the night to night dreams
She's a rose in the greens and a rock out the valley
She gives me happiness with simple things that may not make the world happy
The Love, The Confidence, The Poppy, The Big Daddy
The Comfort, The Support, Damn! It's kind of hard to imagine
Her love with so much passion give me vibes like she's a magnet
I had to brace myself for hurt because this feeling ain't known for lasting
But she is no season or time passing she has more than enough to give and a lot to offer
Educated as I may seem, she challenges her man to become smarter
More than enough qualities for a starter, but patient enough to ride the bench
Cause it's not about her playtime she shows support for her team to win
And at that point I know I had found a friend
Because it wasn't just once she showed loyalty and respect, it was again and again
Challenge by men in the numbers of armies but they won't harm me
Cause the Queen won't allow the King to be lonely when times get stormy, You feel that?
My Baby, no matter how many of her jewels may get misplace, I never trade a good heart and good soul for another body and cute face
And from years to this date, I have stood by her as she has stood by me
Some say I'm just a man but I feel like a King when I'm on the side my Queen

THAT'S LOVE

We have been together for a couple months, but it feels like a few years
Struggled with each other, and some days we shared a few tears
I never feel that you're not here because you always stay close by
We always tell the honest truths and stay away from dark lies
I'm loving your shoe size because you are the only one that can fit it
And you loving on my lifestyle because I'm the only one that can live it
We have them friends like," Yawl did it," because they didn't see it coming
Because when we said we were in love, they thought that we were stunting
Now we stay making moves, on to go, and doing it on a daily basis
Ducking all the haters because it's so easy wanting to see love's failure
Praying we don't make it because they don't want to see us happy
And they double right back and pray that they can have it
Woman wanting to replace you, men wanting to have you
Keeping each other on game is something that we mastered
Because you already have a blessing and I'm feeling real blessed
And love birds always make sure other birds
Don't play around their nest

SOMETHING SPECIAL

I wanted to do something special for you today
So I went to the florist but somehow she was out of roses
So I left to buy some candy, your favorite, but they had just sold them
That was right after I saw a card, but the feelings weren't strong enough
So I went down to the theater, but every movie we already saw
I wanted to take you to dinner, but you told me you'll be little late
And I could have cook you something, but I know you are watching your weight
I refuse to stop right now for seeing that smile upon your face
I went back to the same florist and told her to give me whatever she had
Bought a fresh bag of candy and a funny card to make you laugh
Instead of movie, I got soft music to listen to while we eat
A candlelight dinner with something light
homemade Subway, ham and cheese

WHEN THE HEART IS BIGGER THAN YOUR THOUGHTS,
YOU CAN HAVE A SIMPLE LOVE DATE
THAT RANKS RIGHT OF THE CHARTS
Keep the love flowing

THE STRUGGLE SECTION

THE CYCLE

How dare you break the cycle of beating women and calling them names
How dare you break the cycle of making decisions and giving others the blame
How dare you break the cycle of believing everything the people have to say
How dare you break the cycle of not preparing for tomorrow, just living for today
How dare you break the cycle of holding a child back from reaching their dreams
How dare you break the cycle of making problems worse than what it seems
How dare you break the cycle of believing opinions before knowing all the facts
How dare you break the cycle of going on with your life without looking back
How dare you break the cycle of making family choices based just on yourself
How dare you break the cycle of wanting more love than you willing to give
How dare you break the cycle of wanting to destroy rather than seeing it live
How dare you break the cycle of criticism, discrimination, and racism
How dare you break the cycle of wealth being the prime purpose of living

HOW DARE YOU BREAK THE CYCLE ……

NO

I DARE YOU BREAK THE CYCLE

THE JOURNEY

Have you forgotten
This journey has not ended but has started
The truth lies beneath the feet of a man who chose to seek
The world for the love of his own happiness
Day by day, night by night, he chooses to follow the star
That shines upon him from within, nor does he loses or win
For the completion of his pattern
But for the honor of himself because people say it seems a challenge
Only great ones have conquered, only true believers achieve
But I have already seen it so there is no future in waiting to see it
The rain has passed, how can I treat myself so unhealthy
There's no need for clocks I want let time outlast me
My bravery, my courage won't let me do so
Eye to eye with a familiar face that ready, set, go
Please go, for God sake, you are a man
So many reasons to fall, but too many reasons to stand
How can I gain, If I'm constantly taking losses?
But how can I go wrong when I'm in control of making all my choices
If its poison that slows you down, we'll let energy be the cure
It's ok to give credit for your support, but it started with you that got you here
You're a survivor and one day, the life lessons of the world
You will willingly give
To teach the world of a life
You learned to live

THAT'S LIFE

Do you have any idea how many times you wanted to give up on life
Call it a day, end it at night, with feelings that it was right
Cause my money was tight and right now I don't know who love me
But I feel this picture can't get no better so why not make it more ugly
You have no idea what it is like to be single out, have doubts, and live without support
And there is no one else for me to count on, so there is nowhere else is for me to go
Being broke is one thing but to go without is another
Like love from family and support from my mother
Everyday its struggle since small I been praying for change
So a person felt sorry for me and put a couple coins in my hand
And thankful for the consideration but where on God's Earth is that so called one nation
The lack of participation from higher authority kills minority
We crying for help and our children are getting slaughter
Life is getting harder and my people are really tired
Grandmother slaved her whole life and Daddy just got fired
Hoodlums have desires to start gangs to have love and respect
Schools corrupted and that lack of guidance leads to death
For us to get through we going to have to stick together take effect
But they say that's just a myth, it's crab in the barrel when you Black
The facts, We All Matter, to make change I'll sacrifice
To rise for mankind because this isn't living but I guess it's life

SELF INCACERATED

So many downplay it on how I made it through the hardest times of my life
When my doubts was at its highest and everything wasn't going upright
And my sight was as blurry as driving on a foggy night
Battling them same daily situations but daily losing the fight
But everything would be alright if I just can get this plan to fall through
Because I had no more time to wait in line for their dreams and goals to come true
But the more I thought I realize it wasn't worth it
How this season would come again so there was no need to ballin early
So, I'll never forget that Thursday when I learn how to exercise my mind, body, and soul
Reading books, working out, staying indoors just to keep control
For a world that wasn't ready for my presence and to avoid all those times, I miss my blessings
And so many guessing that it was easy when they see me
But so many prayers upstairs the demons had to free me
And please believe it, that its worth every second, minute, struggle, pain and tear
Cause through self-incarceration I was able to stand as a man living life without the fear
So, no matter what tomorrow bring my way
I still be standing here

WHAT MAKES YOU DIFFERENT

He asked me, "What Makes You Different?"
And I was ready to explain if he was ready to listen
As I explain my life invention
Not under the intentions to persuade but to pave way for those who can't escape
When it came to food, I had no plate so what was given was what I eat
Not saying they left me to starve but it wasn't need or want it was leave or take
Habituating with tigers and snakes known as a predator but seen as a prey
No matter what door I opened for myself it was closed before I could enter the way
The artist paints me in grey to show the emotion as I proceed the ocean
How dare I drown myself but to carry the load was part of the motion
With no sight I kept my focus, so my life, I fixed and repaired on daily
To quit was not an option because they would try to save me
They phrase me "a Loser" throwing rocks but I keep on walking
Because I leave up to others to be statistics of prisons and coffins
So officer, when you asked me, "What makes me different from all the others?"
I'll let you decide cause I see in your eyes you think we all the same by gender and color

SEA ME

They have placed me on the beach to teach
The sand that the water can't reach
How to still feel unique
As the sun shines on them both taking notes
Eager to be apart of the mist, some things you can still miss
No one gets a grip of the smooth texture its something special
The way we build our castles out of clay is cliché
For if that water comes to close our dreams can be washed away
As we lay enjoying the rays to get red
We pillow our bodies in comfort in it, as it give resembles of our bed
Looking over our heads, colorful spaceships travel in the wind
Just to land and mark its spot but the spot soon disappears
You can be any shape you want to be long as your smile is big
Unwind in time feel free to let go of that wig
There's no danger here just a view of raw talents
You can sink your mind beyond, but your feet keeps you balance
So here the challenge for the water that the sand cannot reach
Hold on to every creature and share love throughout the whole beach
Successfully the sand can finally feel what it see
Beach-lieve It !!

FATHER FIGURE

My girl told me a story I couldn't envision
On how a man could make the decision Not to be there
But he care enough to have it rough and stuff her with his goody
Figuring he caring himself like a man because he keeps a pistol under his hoodie
But he just a rookie to simple and plain to understand
That she only going to do the best she can, but it takes a man to raise a man
I cry in pain wishing that this wasn't a real sitcho
Because too many little boys looking like girls because their father not in picture
Wondering if my baby mother feel like I'm less than a daddy figure
Cause no matter how much money I send and how many time I call
If you aren't there to guide like you provide, you really not giving your all
And I took my charge but sometimes it hard dealing with reality
So every time I see a man who has the opportunity he doesn't take it saddens me
The ignorance the excuses he constantly uses
Forcing the mother to work overtime in love to cover up the broken hearted bruises
The choices we choosing I thought was going to break the cycle and make a difference
Instead we lead them on and cheer them on right to coffins and prisons
What's your mission, man? Are you a man on a mission
Cause I will not watch my child life be ended so I will be there in the beginning
There when they are losing there and when they are winning
But I'll be there! Because I am a proud father figure

WHY DID YOU VOTE?

They ask me why did I vote
Like they didn't know change was going to come a difference was going to be made
That we were no longer separated by master or by slave
That the road that use to be rock and gravel is getting cemented to be paved
Or how King, is smiling right now, because his dream being lived, despite he dead
They ask me why did I take the time to vote
Like they didn't know how hard my people fought day and night
Sacrifice after sacrifice, all the beating to have these rights
Sticking together for better so one day my future could be bright
So I paid them back this morning when I walk upon that voting site
They ask me, "Why did you vote"
And this time I made them think
About all the suffering and pain of 9/11 and the war in Iraq
For the families with broken hearts of the soldiers we can't get back
For the economy going down and gas prices going on the rise
It came to a time that we have taken all we can bare
We no longer needed just a president we needed someone who cared
So I took my determination and faith to God despite all the drama
And on 11/04/2008 was the day of our 1st African American President Barrack Obama

WE ARE ONE

I noticed every time we get together, the attitudes of my family get no better
Somehow we find the fuel that starts the fire
Displaying others situations and problems like we ain't got none
Only because we family it doesn't turn violent, but I ask myself is it worth it
It's cool to have fun and games but what's the purpose
Can anyone of you interpret what the Justice?
When it's just us who fuss amongst each other sister and brother, brother and cousin
And you call that Love?
So we separate and fail to educate the upcoming youth about the truth
Cause it's the roots that hold us together
And what's a better time than now to make things better
Let death be a lesson
That tomorrow may be too late to show the gratitude of the ones you love so great
Let's participate in making the weak strong build around the backbone
So the family legacy can live on
Because I ask again how long we going to stay divided?
Physical we are here together, but mentally we still ain't got it
And honest I love you all
So making my contribution today cause I couldn't wait until tomorrow
With the feeling of sorrow that you have a choice to think not
But we are one, we are family, and most important we all we got

SUCCESS SECTION

I'M READY TO GO

You like here
Cause I'm ready to go
Is this the last place you
taking me
Cause I'm ready to go
I understand you want to rest a little
But I'm ready to go
I don't want to leave you behind
But I'm ready to go
This is not a cool place to chill
I'm ready to go
I don't want to hang around misery and sorrow
I'm ready to go
I don't like hearing people complaining.
I'm ready to go
Cause if you want to take me somewhere
Take me to happiness
Take me to joy
Take me to success
Take me to prosperity
Why?
Because I'm ready to go !!

RAIN RAIN RAIN

Rain rain rain shower me with Blessings
Rain Rain Rain joy I feel your presence
Rain Rain Rain how beautiful you fall
Rain Rain Rain I'm growing standing tall
Rain Rain Rain I hear it in the Thunder
Rain Rain Rain you make me wonder
Rain Rain Rain I dance to your music
Rain Rain Rain you are my Cupid
Rain Rain Rain pour for all my friends
Rain Rain Rain rinse my soul again
Rain Rain Rain your light electric strike
Rain Rain Rain it really shook me right
Rain Rain Rain I'm ready to fully blossom
Rain Rain Rain all I see is prosper
Rain Rain Rain I feel younger but getting older
Rain Rain Rain my cup is running over

I AM A PUBLIC FIGURE

I'm the great never late
Make it better, change this place
My distinguished looks you can't ignore it
I'm well-built and designed to be heroic
Brains full of intelligence no negligence
Just evidence of greatness all I ever been
And ever since I acknowledge my knowledge
I have been dust free, I can polish the polished
Give me the power I pushing the facts
They took it away, now I am taking it back
I been giving poor, since I was living check to check
I created jobs, and I never sold no crack
I'm bringing it back , its greener on the other side
I take pride in who I am, I swear not to tell one lie
I stand tall and won't shy, I'm getting things right don't you cry, there's better days and better nights
I'm here to make a major difference
I work harder than hard despite my pension
I'm an the invention that the world never know it would see
I am a Public Figure you can Vote for me
Successful we will be

BLESSED NO PRETENDING

Blessed no pretending
I'm extending my wealth
I fear no disease
But conscious of health
I journey my life so I'm running with self
I'm boxing a good fight holding the belt
A King among Kings the cards I was dealt
A pray to God on my knees
And he answered every time that I knelt
Blessings My soul never cold Like told
I got a body full riches my gold pure gold
Behold so much greatness is among us
We lightning every room and speaking through the thunder
The Team we are seeing dreams through every vision
It's A Winning Season, I foresee forever winning with no ending
I'm Blessed no Pretending

LIFEGOODENERGY

I'm life good energy
I have no enemies
So even if you envy me
Your negativity will not enter me
Vision me I behold good source
In my oath, I spoke my love will make you float
Give me your vote and let me give you support
This is not a race
This is a get up lets go
I imagine what you imagine could happen
But only your actions can change the caption
Relying on the pastor is past tense
I'm straight connected to God
I'm but to cash in
I life good energy
My name became a brand
When my pops gave me the initials but my mom birth a man
And they introduce me to God and my life hasn't been the same
Because despite my peanut butter skin
I been getting out every jam
Let me help you understand
My faith isn't fiction so my work got me winning
Success I will forever see and this only the beginning
I more than just trending and I never blend with a crowd
To much peace not to smile
So don't you lie to that child
You can be whatever you want to be
I am LifeGoodenergy

AT PEACE

I can eat I can sleep
I'm at peace
You can see that I am free
I'm at peace
I can be what I want to be
I'm at peace
I can ride I can fly
I'm at peace
When it storms, I am calm
I'm at peace
When it harm I'm alarmed
I'm at peace
When it's broke, I can fix
I'm at peace
When doors close, I can open
I'm at peace
There nothing wrong with seeing right
I'm at peace
My view is bright even during at night
I'm at peace

A GIPHTED STORY

A real untold story
And if the world never know me God still gets the glory
And as I do my inventory my blessings have been blessed
My tests have been test
But I'm never stressed cause I play chess
I am Giphted
A Multitasking soulmate up early working late
I don't eat if my children haven't ate
I go harder than hard so they can play
I'm talking about stocks and leaving a safe
I am Giphted
Denied delayed but not afraid to go ahead
I go dough to dough 364 because it takes just 1 day to see the bread
I am Giphted
My soul flow through the bodies of everybody who so excited to have the talents and skills
To go through life drills and drama making their periods commas
Here is my truth your honor
I die in honor with persona saying your troubles have been lifted
In life, I have piece my own puzzle I am Giphted

THE JOURNEY OF SEXY TRIO

Sexy trio is a sequel
Made up of lovely and beautiful people
Where the understanding is always understood
And if the hour glass is half way we will always see the Good
Rising each other like the old neighborhood where everyone plays their part
Failure has no place we will always make the mark
There a reason to the season that our greatness come this far
Because we won't deny the signs of present times Noah and his ark
Heavenly thoughts keeps us spark and our fires burns high
There is much of us on earth as we smiling at the sky
People tears of for the cry but our tears of for the growth
Psalms in every song and joy in every note
Always sign of hope strength and courage
Famous quote is "I love it "
As private as we live our faith is always seen so public
There is not a touchy subject that we can touch
And there's not a quality time we will rush
Where much is required much is given
Where much is spoken much is listen
So continue to fly high and soar like eagles
And continue to smile this story sequels
The words of a journeyman
"If we journey now, then we will journey then

LOVE THE TEAM

I love the team like I love a queen
First thing I tell her is follow your dreams
Despite what it may seem your beauty makes you a beast
I not sure what they see but they will see
The strength the courage and the ability to endless win over defeat
Even when life cheat, we will take a stand for a Rosa Parks seat
Unique conquering all big and small
Them slips trips and falls help us rise tall
You can minimize who you call
If you know how to call on God
Because life ain't that hard if you not dog in the fire
But have the fire in the dog
Pause, breathe, believe, and achieve
We have to heal from all the hurt that made us grieve
Turn the pain into pleasure
And know your success is not measured
By the riches, friends switching, and family poor comprehension
And I did I mention you very smart
You don't have to crawl, you can walk
You don't have to walk, you can march
But in order to finish, you have to start
I love the team with all my heart
I want to see you shine
I want to see you smile
The time is now

I Wanna Thank You

There is so much appreciation I have for you! My greatness and my journey became apart of yours. We have explored the world depths and found out how deep life and people can be. And there's no doubt in mind the encouragement needed to continue has already been put in place. The love has be demonstrated and the choices has been made for more happiness to come. Let peace really be with you and know all the stars have line up in your favor. There not any concern or worry from me knowing you will be fine. Your headed to the next level.

www.ingramcontent.com/pod-product-compliance
Lightning Source LLC
LaVergne TN
LVHW010123170826

845678LV00012B/2564

* 9 7 8 1 7 3 6 5 3 8 9 2 0 *